BEING SAFE WITH WEATHER

BY SUSAN KESSELRING • ILLUSTRATED BY DAN McGEEHAN

Published by The Child's World®
1980 Lookout Drive • Mankato, MN 56003-1705
800-599-READ • www.childsworld.com

ACKNOWLEDGMENTS
The Child's World®; Mary Berendes, Publishing Director
The Design Lab: Design and production
Red Line Editorial: Editorial direction

LIBRARY OF CONGRESS CATALOGING-IN-PUBLICATION DATA
Kesselring, Susan.
Being safe with weather / by Susan Kesselring;
illustrated by Dan McGeehan.
    p. cm.
Includes bibliographical references and index.
ISBN 978-1-60954-374-7 (library bound: alk. paper)
1. Storms—Juvenile literature. 2. Weather protection—Juvenile
literature. 3. Weather—Physiological effect—Juvenile literature.
I. McGeehan, Dan, ill. II. Title.
QC941.3.K47 2011
613.69—dc22

                                    2010040479

Printed in the United States of America
Mankato, MN
December, 2010
PA02069

About the Author

Susan Kesselring loves
children, books, nature, and
her family. She teaches K-1
students in a progressive
charter school down a little
country lane in Castle Rock,
Minnesota. She is the mother
of five daughters and lives
in Apple Valley, Minnesota,
with her husband, Rob, and a
crazy springer spaniel named
Lois Lane.

About the Illustrator

Dan McGeehan spent his
younger years as an actor,
author, playwright, and
editor. Now he spends his
days drawing, and he is
much happier.

Hi! I'm Buzz B. Safe. Watch for me! I'll tell you how to have fun and be safe with weather.

W

hat do you do in different kinds of weather? Do you splash in rain puddles or tumble in the snow? On a hot afternoon, do you eat a cold ice cream cone? You can enjoy nature's weather— rain or shine. Just remember to follow some rules and you'll stay safe.

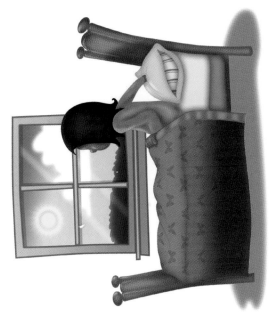

Rain waters plants and fills rivers, lakes, and streams. But too much rain can cause floods. A river's water can spill over onto the land around it.

Listen to a radio or watch television if heavy rain is falling. You'll find out if there is a flood warning by your home.

If a flood is near, go to higher ground. Do not try to wade or swim in floodwater. You never know how deep the water is. It could be moving faster than you think, too.

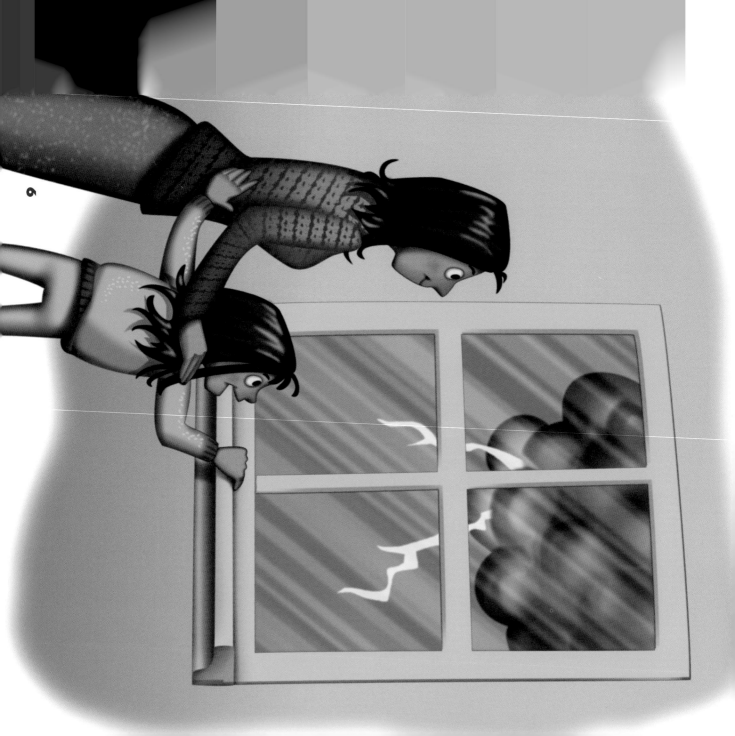

Sometimes thunder and lightning come along with rain. It's a thunderstorm!

A thunderstorm is amazing to see—with its bright flashes and loud cracks. But always watch it from inside a building. If lightning strikes the building, you will still be safe.

During a thunderstorm, don't use a phone with a cord. Don't touch other electronics, like televisions, that have cords. Lightning can come inside through wires.

A thunderstorm that brings large **hail** and strong winds is a severe thunderstorm. It could even include a **tornado**. This type of weather can **damage** buildings and homes.

In a severe thunderstorm or tornado, take cover. Go to the lowest level of your home to wait it out. Make sure you stay away from windows.

If you need to go into the basement, bring a flashlight and a radio with batteries. Grab a game, too. You can play it while you wait for the storm to end. It will be fun, and the time will pass by quickly!

Near the ocean, you might see a different kind of storm—a **hurricane**. If a hurricane reaches land, its wild winds can blow trees and signs over. Hurricane winds travel faster than a car travels on a highway. That's why it's important to stay inside a strong building during a hurricane.

During a hurricane, the ocean at the shore can rise about 20 feet (6 m). If this happens you may have to leave your home until it passes. Your parents will know a safe place where you can go.

Brr! It's snowing. Do you like to build snowmen in the snow? Make sure you stay warm and cozy. Bundle up with a jacket, snow pants, a scarf, mittens, and boots. And don't forget your hat!

Wearing these things will keep you from getting **frostbite**. When you begin to shiver or feel very tired, it's time for you to go inside and warm up.

It's lots of fun to go sledding in the winter! But remember to play safely. Don't sled on ice or near roads. Have a parent watch you, too.

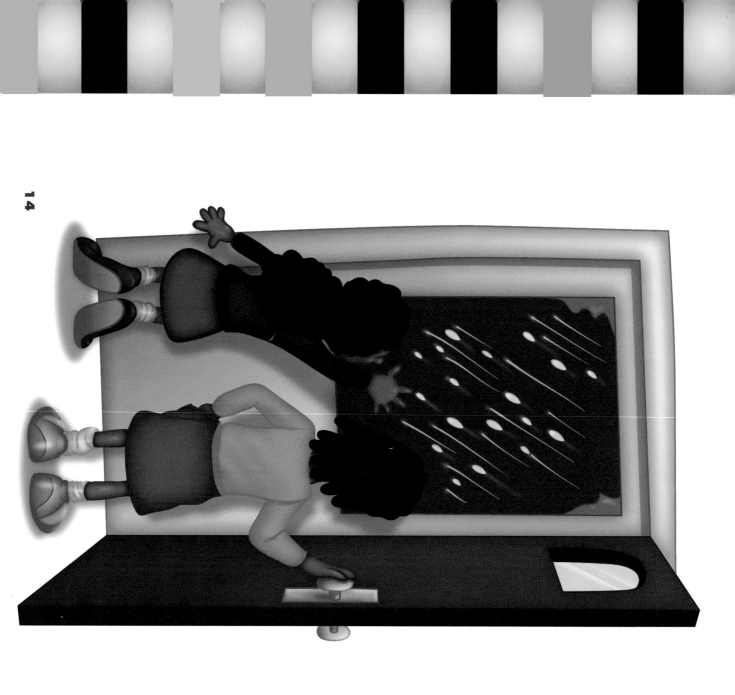

A **blizzard** usually means school is closed for the day. But ask an adult first if it's safe to play outside.

It's easy to get lost outside during a blizzard. Winds blow at speeds more than 35 miles (56 km) per hour. That's faster than your parent drives his or her car through a small town. The blowing snow makes it hard to see even a few feet in front of you.

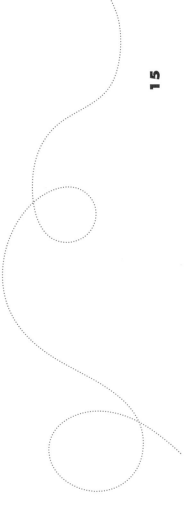

What about when the weather turns muggy and hot? Do you ride a bike and play tag? It's fun to play outside in summer, but remember a few rules.

Drink lots of cold liquids.

Wear clothing that keeps you cool, such as shorts and tank tops. Also, stay in the shade as much as you can.

Swimming in a pool or a lake is a great way to cool off. Just make sure there is an adult to watch you swim. And, don't forget to wear sunscreen!

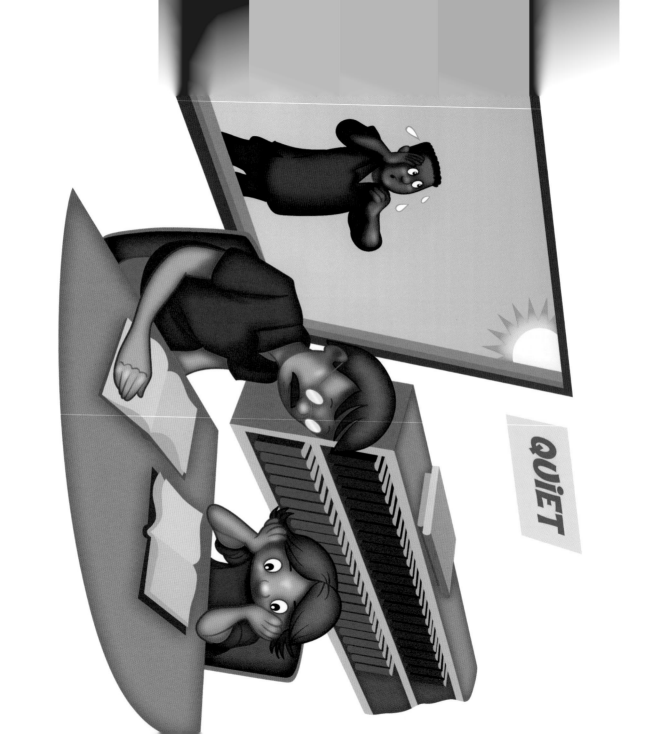

QUIET

Some days it is just too hot! You could get very sick if you ran around outside.

Stay inside your home and keep the air conditioning on. If your home doesn't have air conditioning, spend some time at a cool library reading a good book. Or visit a friend's house and play board games.

Remember to always keep an eye to the sky. And check out the **weather report** to learn what weather is headed your way. That will keep you safe—indoors and out!

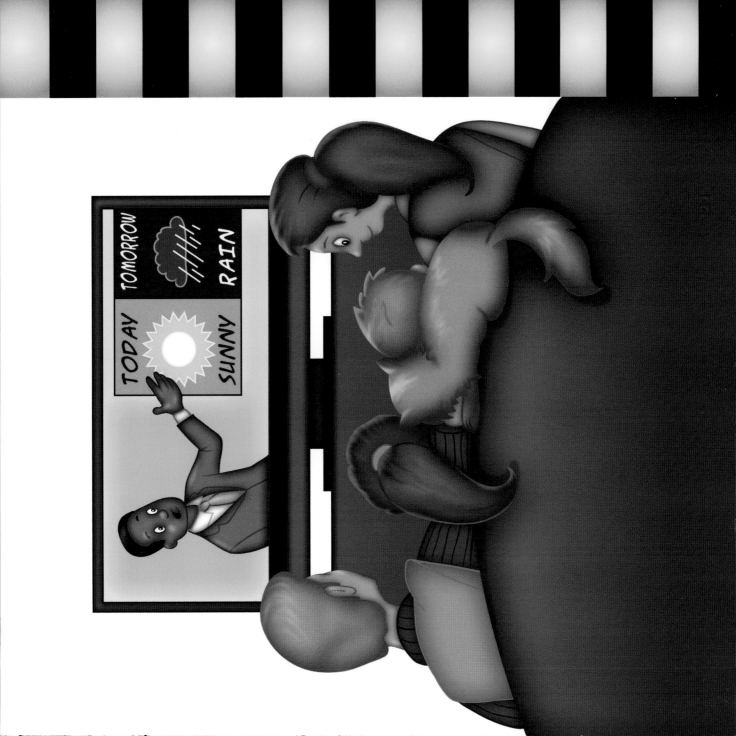

WEATHER SAFETY RULES
TO REMEMBER

1. Pay attention to the weather report.

2. If you hear thunder or see lightning, go inside a house or a building.

3. During a tornado or a severe thunderstorm, go to the lowest level of your home and stay away from windows.

4. Don't wade or try to swim in flooded areas, including rivers, creeks, or streets.

5. In hot weather, drink a lot of water and wear light, loose clothing.

6. In cold weather, bundle up!

Always be safe!

GLOSSARY

blizzard (BLIZ-urd): A blizzard is a winter storm with strong wind, heavy snow, and cold temperatures. You may not be able to play outside during a blizzard.

damage (DAM-ij): To damage something means to break or ruin it. A tornado or a hurricane can damage buildings.

frostbite (FRAWST-byt): Frostbite is an injury to the skin caused by cold temperatures. Stay bundled up in cold weather so you don't get frostbite.

hail (HAYL): Hail is small balls of ice that fall from the sky. A severe thunderstorm can bring hail.

hurricane (HUR-uh-kayn): A hurricane is a storm with high winds that forms over an ocean. If a hurricane is coming, you may need to leave your home for safer shelter.

tornado (tor-NAY-doh): A tornado is a spinning tunnel of air that reaches from the clouds to the ground. Take cover in a basement or a strong building during a tornado.

weather report (WETH-ur ri-PORT): A weather report is a news report that tells what the weather will likely be. Listen to or watch the weather report to see if it's okay to play outside.

TO LEARN MORE

BOOKS

Johnson, Jinny. *Being Safe.* New York: Crabtree Publishing, 2010.

Macken, JoAnn Early. *Waiting Out the Storm.* Somerville, MA: Candlewick Press, 2010.

Simon, Seymour. *Weather.* New York: Collins, 2006.

WEB SITES

Visit our Web site for links about being safe with weather:

childsworld.com/links

Note to Parents, Teachers, and Librarians: We routinely verify our Web links to make sure they are safe and active sites. So encourage your readers to check them out!